Frantzy Civil's

Wider Perspectives Publishing ¤ 2024 ¤ Hampton Roads, Va.

The poems and writings in this book are the creations and property of Frantzy Civil, the author is responsible for them as such. Wider Perspectives Publishing reserves 1st run rights to this material in this form, all rights revert to author upon delivery. Author reserves all rights thereafter: Do not reproduce without permission except Fair Use practices for approved promotion or educational purposes. Author may redistribute, whole or in part, at will, for example submission to anthologies or contests.

© 2024, Frantzy Civil, including writing as Civil, Frantzy
1st run complete in August 2024
Wider Perspectives Publishing, Hampton Roads, Va.
ISBN 978-1-964531-09-0

Contents

First Find Love
                    2
Emotionally Locked
                    6
Damage Done   Part 1
                    8
Dear Destroyers
                    10
Emotionally Locked ... Continues
                    14
S.T.U.P.I.D. Can Be
                    16
Damage Done   Part 2
                    20
Unfortunate Flake
                    22
Broken Glass
                    24
Mad at You... Why?
                    26
Damage Done   Part 3
                    28
X-Tasee'
                    30
All Aboard.All Welcome In
                    34

Frantzy Civil

First Find Love

What is love.., baby don't hurt me..,
Don't hurt me.., no more

Actually, please hurt me some more
Baby, for real please I need to feel every bit of that pain
Throbbing, rushing through your veins
Arteries, coming from those heart aching years
Searching for that guy thinking it was me,
            but I only left you crippling in tears
See, I don't think Truly I have love for myself enough
Letting all that time pass, and still, I wasn't enough
Love is blind it can take over your mind
But first you need to celebrate what you have before you can find
That hidden secret that lies in your spine
Meaning: If you don't have a great foundation
You'll have your mind wandering in time
Caught up in the *hijee beejees* wasting precious moments dabbling
Coming up with tricks and schemes because you want to shine
But all those years instead of building
         you were stuck thinking how it can be
            and what could have been
Wait, I already said so much,
        man that's not where I even wanted to begin
First find love, in yourself and breathe it in
Understand humans are devilish,
         but nature has a way of teaching us
           through trials and tribulations,
     honestly have no idea why I started the poem singing
            this song by Haddaway
What Is Love, asking not to be hurt anymore with his heart crying
It's touching, very uplifting in many ways, but also sickening

Watching a grown man crying his heart out to a woman
To not be hurt by her, when nature shows
        that a man's more logical then emotional
Lead her, not follow her; relying on you to guide the missile
Listen if the mind crumbles logically
        it doesn't matter how much love you have
Celine Dion realizes love is caring for one another
        based on what is needed
Not faking it because you want to abuse the kindness
        of a person as weakness
But realizing in yourself at some point
        you may have to indulge that same weakness:
        feeling defeated
Some people feel the need to hold somebody else's emotions
        and mind in captivity
Trying to psychologically and financially chain them
        to capture them
Some just need somebody to fill in that gap
        because of the guilt and shame
Yeah, I'm talking to you, it's sad because you might be loosing
        somebody truly valuable to you
We are not flourishing and building each other for good
        based on our passions, goals, skills and talents
We try to see ways we can take advantage
        because we are on a deep inside level broken
A wise man said all is self,
So why am I so insecure, or hateful towards myself
The world will continue to beat me down
        like a turtle hiding under my shell
Let those resentments, hateful, fearful vibrations I learned
        and was conditioned to move away from myself
See, love is something between pain and pleasure where
Usually most of us not truly cherishing ourselves,
        hearts passions and goals will suffer

Frantzy Civil

Love is infinite possibilities of strong desirable feelings
                      that can get overwhelming
That same energy can push-out hates, resentment to fill your world
But to me if you truly love somebody you'll be honest
Truthful as you can be
Why… Communication is key
Because Love is karma, universe sending you
                      what you're vibrating subconsciously
Because consciously most are hiding their true intentions secretly
It's only a matter of time, I suggest you speed it up
                      to know and realize that quickly
Although the universe gives freely,
                      there's a lot to learn in nature, truly
But as humans it can be detrimental to our being
                      – if not deadly
Just like watching porn, jerking off, you're stroking your ego
                      for a temporary feeling
Not content with who you are in your own skin
I used to feel bad about masturbating,
                      thinking it's the devil or something
                      overpowering me, touching me,
                      using my hands to stroke my thing
Based on the religion I was raised in, technically
                      if I don't repent or feel ashamed
I'll be going to Hell, burning the impurities away
                      before I can reach Heaven
I can't deny they might have some influence,
                      but most of us gradually dig our own graves
Longing, stressing, worrying, and jumping into a dark state,
                      crying out to God asking to be saved
Trying to shed off that agonizing pain we all
                      knowingly or unknowingly
                          living in

It's not good or bad… there's consequence
        in depleting one's energy without regaining balance
The more you put into something the more you'll receive,
                that's not by chance
Remember, holding strong emotions towards your goals
        – passions and desires will enhance
How soon it manifests depends upon the
        time and energy spent doing it – that's science
Stop wondering and go find love,
    but where does one start?
    In yourself first
to get out the illusions and suspense.

Frantzy Civil

Emotionally Locked

It feels like the is world crumbling upon me,
Like I've been locked for decades behind bars,
How can that be…?
Being that my spirit is keeping me away
               from getting any prison scars!
It's fascinating honestly,
Although, many occasions I've come close to make it that far,
Yes, I've spend time in the county jail cells, precincts and all
In this body I am using so far,
One of the main objectives in this game is staying away
               from breaking these laws
I live a life that aggravates most people's personal flaws
Sometimes knowing me is like struggling to climb a brick wall
I feel and sense your pain, the squeaking crawl of your nails
               trying not to fall…
Any further into unwanted circumstances like a snowball
I see where you're going but if it is not logical I block off for sure
If you're pushing your fuckery upon me I retreat into myself more
It can be detrimental sometimes
       which is one of the reasons we engage in wars..,
With ourselves, peers, parents and all
Targeting each other's emotions, moods, psyche and all
From different aspects, levels and spheres!
Many are conditioned to worry with fear!

First,

Forcing to plot against each other
            for the sake of becoming a 'bourgeoisie'
At times I feel emotionally torn while maintaining
               a relationship with unlawfulness
Keeping myself alive
            for the primary purpose of richness
From a seemingly motherless child climbing past my twenties
Graduated the teenagers stage, now all grown up
              with goals & enemies
Not truly comprehending my enemies are my inner-me(s)
That needs to be check & balance
            so one don't get left with liabilities
In a state of violence death and prison
              is the most common possibilities
It is through my own demise I am suffering freely
Disregarding my heart's passions have inflict great injuries,
To the point where I might be emotionally locked,
           engaging in situations that diminish me

Damage Done
Part 1

I don't know why it feels like I have been wrestling a crocodile
Simply from losing a job, moving out to changing my hairstyle
Days later the girl I'm with told me to excuse her for a while
Why? she needs some time off to go look at the other aisles
She haven't return,
                 & since then like a felon running away from trial
I can't blame her for hiding these awkward feelings like a child
The way I move in the air seems foul
Birds eye view, but I keep my emotions to myself in a pile
Where we stand with each other now
                        is somewhere between faith and exile
Hey, it can be stressful
                   getting complicated with a woman too soon
Eventually emotions get entangled and soon,
Followed by numerous switches of her moods,
And; I can't be there as much as I should
Although she knows I'm dealing with something
                           I can't be there like I would
May be 5 years ago we would have been good
Before I became misunderstood
                  followed by a series of misfortunes,
But nevermind those tunes
Girl, I love you far beyond Jupiter's moons

Frantzy Civil

Dear Destroyers

Dear destroyers and conquerors of many nations...
We know all your plans are full
                of deceiving tricks for destruction...
Through many schematics of politics which keeps us
                in a state of division and confusion.
We are not here to ask for piece, we know the pie
                has already gone into distribution,
Ain't no piece left, nor was there any piece intended on given
                during the decision!
We are not the only ones that have been struck down
                for our skin tone and complexions,
Most of the others have already been subdued
                under your cruel intentions.
Go ahead categorize me as another black boy
                crying for pension!
We know this system is being controlled and designed
                by slave owners since then...
So will there ever be any real change!?
It seems like you'll always have a problem whenever we speak
                with passion...
To exercise our, so called rights as a human
                in order to function,
When it comes to fixing ourselves and our situations...
Wanting more like Noble Ju Ali might have you'll say,
                "fuck the constitution!"
Depriving us from being a nation
                through economic depression!

That's why,
Generations after generations you'll make it your mission...
Before and after Dr. King, and Malcolm,
To reprocess the same type of killing and tyranny.
The real change is governments became better at hiding
          the filth and waste of bodies,
But the pile is hitting the fan now it's getting messy!
After many centuries of crimes now the odor
          is increasing tremendously,
With the information being passed outside it is getting
          a little windy...
We are seeing more and more of your dogs running loose
          violently attacking anybody!
I sometimes wonder if different television networks
          are staging this publicly...
Is it hate truly,   or Tom foolery..?
You know getting each other mad being playful and silly
Hey, because after all we are one big human family
I haven't totally grasped it seems like you all deliberately
          do things to get us angry?
                    (But why would that be?)
To profess a civil war, where it becomes
          another game being played by the elites...
You see, perfect timing for conglomerations
          of big businesses that have enough money!
Another opportunity to stump or put a knee
          on the competition's neck,
Many of you will do anything in this game to gain respect!
The majority of us love people for being people
          without discriminating any sect,

Frantzy Civil

A baby isn't born to hate, as a child he or she
                is groomed into this mess!
The media is only here to trump us down, pump racism
                into our chest,
Turning suffering into a comedy, to the point I don't know
                if I'm crazy or just have PTSD!
Emotions change drastically,
            from overwhelming excitement of anger
                to being depressed,
Finding joy laughing at our own misery
                although we are deeply stressed
Blocking our natural feelings to feel sorrow and pain
                for people and the rest...
Mmmh let me say less, let me say less!
But it's mind boggling when you'll be spoiling pigs
            for taking advantage shooting us
            like exterminators killing pests!
Are you all being rewarded to make it seem like an accident
                to purposely destroy our lives!?
Some might describe it as animalistic, racism, devilish,
            and all in between the lies.
It seems like the revolution is already being televised,
            like an action movie on syfy...
Are we all truly here waiting for the same happy ending...
                                      Why!?
Injustice being overly expressed is the only suitable role
              we have ever been given,
Still being treated like babies, but how come
              you don't love us the same!?
How come we aren't kept properly safe and
              receive the same information!?

Although we can create our own movie
                        instead of the frustrations...
Our schizophrenic minds are ignorant
          of you using agonizing and terrorizing tactics
                                      for separation,
Keeping most of us repeatedly going through
                the same loop of distortion
In the state of fear and anxiety, it's easy to
                lose our concentration
So, what the hell do you all think I'm supposed to be doing..?

Frantzy Civil

Emotionally Locked ...
Continues

With more time I let set upon this abnormality
The more I acquire and engage in some type of dis-ease
The more it'll spread and fester entertaining it you see
That is why it is necessary to concentrate
                and see goals as clear as water
Like seagulls flying & nesting around the coastal shores
                not going any further
Simply enjoying what they have around as food
                and amusement without any diversity
It's ironic they usually live together in large,
                densely packed, noisy colonies
Similar to humans but I don't know if we are living in harmony…
Nor are we moving with trusting personalities
It'll be nice if we all organize together
                to prevent certain incidents & injuries
But we rather cause each other harm for real
While mentally scheming taking advantage
                of each other's identities

In this gorgeous, horrible world we as humanity
Can agree that we are losing because of tyranny
When we do an in-depth study of history
We can say those so called in control are diabolical
                in every way possible

Doesn't matter how vicious the plan or idea may seem
                         as long as it is suitable
For the ultimate improvement of society
Where those that are suffering is necessary
I guess at the same time we are building something beautiful
                         with all this technology
Even if the food is toxic/poisonous
            slowly depleting the human families, sht..,
It won't be a conundrum to say..,
I'll have what she's having... misery/pain
                    on top of this cherry sundae
            Okay!!!
And also; don't forget an extra spoon for the tears today
Or a cloth I haven't decide if I want to wipe it away
Why usually the tears are hard to tear up the tear-ducts
                    and fall away
But today it seems like they want to do
                  'the Michael Jordan's fade away'
Which I still can't even fully explain why
At this point I am wondering should I even try
Sometimes I laugh so much that I cry
But it isn't funny noticing financial abusement of others
                    in disguise, in the sky
Although many of us spirits have dye and die
Masquerading or disregarding what I am is to hide
Like a box of chocolate
I'll say it's best to savor your time and make it worthwhile

Frantzy Civil

S.T.U.P.I.D. Can Be

For a large portion in my life I felt like a 'Smart, Tormented,
Uplifting, Peaceful, Ignominious, Dummy'.

That is what I was running on, you don't want to find out
how stupid I can be
It seems like I can't get nothing right,
not knowing what was left undone is haunting me
I don't know how a good source of energy
that can guide me out of foolery
Allah, God, Buddah or whichever is the one and only…
Should I just stay there and one of you will
shape the road for me?
Honestly, that doesn't make sense, but what is the force
managing this life?
This bugs me out for decades, scratching my head like I had lice
After going into some experiences once or twice
The main subject reverse to the same usage of spice
There's no difference in religion
Just a difference in the explanations
It's difficult to understand; so many religious dogmas
encrypted in my brain
I will never totally have issues with parents,
we're all being conditioned
I am subconsciously aware, consciously alert
and unconsciously defiant, you see
Life feels like a high stake game of clever intellectuals
in existence here
Some way somehow society, peers and all have put their fingers in
to influence me

Some get treated like kings, queens, or decent human beings
while the others are puppetry
Nowadays, our politicians and the governments
are our celebrities..,
So who were our celebrities back then, say
sometime in the fifties?
Since the foundation of this country
There have been groups of gathers for the purpose
of governing minds
*Hey, listen I'm fine, all I need are the correct resources
and I can govern mine*
We can see it all around as we continue in time
From gangs, to army, to governments even world leaders
Partaking in demolishing for the purpose
of building their own structures
Who reaps the most benefits are high up in the control centers
Although it hurts a lot, prior to the fact that
we have less money to consider...
At this moment I am classified as poor although
my mental is rich, however
The knowledge and information acquired
wasn't being put together...
Properly for the sake of increasing wealth, I was in
a different dimension
I missed that part of the game..,
Parents and Gods couldn't accepts my goals and passion
Maybe I have not realized there is a legacy worth leaving
for my children
Yes, although plenty things are already upside down
and twisted around

Frantzy Civil

If nothing is done, I might find myself trapped
for however long it takes battling the same lesson
Since my days in college I remember
'Proper Preparation Prevents Poor Performance'
Even though when the word 'stupid' is said and applied
in a cool-nice way for the audience
Depends on which and what scenario it is
taking place or mentioned
I couldn't stay joking for too long when my moms
gave me a billion reasons...
To continue on
Moving forward I can only stay with the faith I'm feeling
through the seasons
While working or making more of what matters
which in slang is 'chicken'
For my ancestor's sake I will make it for certain
Even if I am a
"Smart, Tormented, Uplifting,
Peaceful, Ignominious, Dumb'
being

Damage Done
Part 2

If only we had linked up and decided to build something
It wouldn't feel as suffocating…
Like the way I used to choke and strangle my feelings
To the point where I recoil into an introvert and say
    damn I despise these feelings
Like a mute I don't say much about anything
In my cocoon studying myself, now I say so much
    it's like I'm teaching
You became spiteful with me because I say too much things
It's irking to feel like I have to over explain things,
When I know you understand,
Plus, I know you want to be held tight
    going through these emotional strains
It's even more irking,
When you can't be brute enough
    to save me from the embarrassment
You know I am comfortable with you..,
Like my other half I can open up too
You don't know how sad it feels you,
Think I'm nonchalant and insensitive towards you
No lie, mentally my focus was far away from you
Might not be obvious I'm dealing psychologically
    with something, too
As my woman you know you can stop me
    and insert your point of view
As we continue conversing...
Only if you notice how annoyed I am feeling
    like I have to keep on validating!

What we have is a beautiful work in progress
                that demands time and attention
I'm not around breathing, and tasting your love
                so it became a funny situation
Everyday I feel the need to wake up next to you
                in order to function
For at least 12 months I will need access into your bosom
Then we will know for sure where we stand
And I can truly give you a vision of where we are going!
I don't think of you as a safe haven
I just thought you'll be somebody I can count on
                while going through the mayhems
Although, energies are forcing you away I stay reeling you in
I still can't figure out why, but it's fascinating
All the evidence is pointing
Towards the fact that, if I'm doing that much,
                it can only mean one thing
Girl, I love you and I wouldn't mind giving you the ring

Frantzy Civil

Unfortunate Flake

I didn't need to see much, may I say,
                                               under your cardigan drape
I can tell you have an hourglass shape
I'll slowly take time to pierce your heavenly gate
Best believe any obstacles in front of me
                                                       would get eliminated
You are a real black jewel; nothing about you seems fake
I apologize for the inconvenient flake…
Time is of the essence for real my girl soul would quake
I have no idea how much her world would break
Although me and you want to manifest our sexual cravings
                                                            past foreplay
I let it slide and also missed a possible three play
Mmmh mmh – I'm not joking but,
it's ironic we got so in-tune in such a short-play
That we wouldn't mind swinging lightly away
Although me and her claimed to be open may I say
Since she wasn't with the lifestyle, it's unfortunate
                                                                 I had to stop it
Because one or all of us would have been devastated
Either way, I sincerely apologize for the time wasted
Although we would enjoy having fun with each other all day
It wasn't my playground
I'll say, the only regret is I can't rewind time
                                                       to rearrange the play
Reminiscing on the fact there was a genuine connection
                                                         that can't be re-played

Frantzy Civil

Broken Glass

Babe, I know I can't have you back
I let you slip and shattered like a broken artifact
The price is enormous to gain you back
The only way to move is forward like a fucking broken glass…
There's no need to dwell onto the past
I comprehend we are unable to fix that,
Even if we want to ignore the fact
               that we have to throw it into the trash
Sweep and pick up the leftovers that might harm the aftermath
         Hey,
The cleaning might not be the best to prevent a scar or a gash
But it soothes me knowing we can walk, move on
               without unknowingly getting slashed
It was my fault mishandling 'the artifact',
               caused it to fall and smash
Irreversible accidents happen, does it mean we wouldn't last?
Being broke or not means nothing, it's how we respond
               to the crash
I'm nonchalant not that I don't want to situate the problem fast
I guess you're not used to that, being calm helps me
               come up with solutions fast
Plus, isn't the respect and love we have for each other
               enough to surpass.!?
(Mmh, I guess not… broken glass..,
We are broken glass)

Frantzy Civil

Mad at You... Why?

You know the saying a wombman has the power to destroy
and/or build a man!
Although emotionally I didn't think or notice
like I was crushing then!
Once I moved in, it didn't take long for you to try
to switch the plans
Now the agony I brought myself wants to keep me chained
Somewhere in a secluded place or basement being tortured
by a psycho being
I don't know how I can intimidate you for the time being!
I don't see a gap where you and I are unable to bridge and
keep what we have sustained!
It's not a rumor; I'm not yet there as of this instance,
Doing the best in organizing what you want to see!
Might not be feeling it as of this instance,
With the low tides, and the calmness, probably!
Or maybe I don't have a vicious domesticated dog
type of mentality!
The way society portrays what status should a man hold
and be, pardon me..!
Might not be where we would like but yeah,
why should I complain?
Let me know what in the world that truly last
without a little pain
Yes, there's a level and different ways of feeling pain
or the idea of pain..!
Yes, I can face the reality, we might unable
to finish building before the rain
With time I am able to find my way to the question
where you get proclaimed
I can't rely on you resisting the distracting faces passing again

You've been pulled here and there by the hands
you called family and friends!
It's my fault giving less of me that I could have give
at the time being
I fail to give you a Jesus or a king figure whom
you can find hope and belief in
I guess what I had offered on the table
was not enough to be valuable
Never mind what could have been it wasn't even mailable
Anyways, forget what is not yet on the table
Nonetheless only thing that is bothering
this so-called heart and brain, boo
I wouldn't mind a lifetime with you
Hey, I guess at least I got a chance to truly know you
Honestly, this wasn't something you're craving,
willing to strive for nor go through!
Never thought I'd be so sick that I feel different being around you.
Although I want and desire you,
And have endless places in mind to experience life with you
Instead I'm here at 3:23AM finishing this poem
in regards to you
Unable to escape this zone and go to la-la-land
for the past few
My mind-ravaging unease with thoughts
since I haven't heard from you
So, yeah, cursing you will only hurt who?
Although I made a decision to better myself
while being with you
I ponder and ask myself, "why should I be mad at you!!?"
Even if communication has a role to play on both sides
of the plain view
It's irrelevant when I knew how you act and still,
I chose to stay with you

Damage Done
Part 3

Depression takes various forms, but it can be mascaraded
That's why for many years I stayed in my solitude dealing with it
Maybe you think I'm broken, miserable,
and can't find somebody to live with..,
I laugh knowing that even if I'm stuck with you
on a deserted Island, I'll love it
I know you're able to read me like I read you
So I let my guard down and chose to feel only you
Sometimes I get intoxicated with thoughts of you
In memory lane watching porn, masturbating, thinking of you
At the same time thinking
maybe I should have kept it strictly sexual with you
Without any string attached *chou-chou*
Like let me know when you need my service,
and I'll do my best to make it there, boo
It's more than that we start having strong feelings for each other,
too,

But the distance was killing us
although there's a way to close that gap
You must know as a man it's my obligation to work out my plans
and follow my map
Get my self situated instead of rushing away
getting caught into a trap
Anything worth fighting for is worth keeping,
but what have I been fighting for?
Have you noticed I've been fighting for your love
to keep me in your life a little bit more!?

There's plenty ways to attend to your sexual
and emotional needs in this store
Be patient, and let me show you
what's on the other side of the door
Love is reciprocal..,

If you aren't doing the same the consequences are irrefutable
I want to share my whole being with you for sure
With a strong bond and sense of empathy we can
go through these obstacles forever more!
It's been many years now since I've spoken of love like this
After I numbed myself and jumped into the abyss
I can honestly say you showed me how to love,
and helped bring my heart justice
From the fears, trauma, and other emotional crises!
As well as the psychological pain I continue to assist
In my life, constantly, I will always thank you
for invigorating this hidden bliss
In my heart, I feel love, and although I've never said it like this!
Girl, I love you and I wouldn't mind taking the risk!

Frantzy Civil

X-Tasee'

You say you're having a terrible day like demons
    are tormenting you
As much as I would love ripping and stripping
    those spirits off of you
While you're crawling off the wall & bed trembling waiting
    for me to pound the ghosts out of you
We don't need no liquor baby to extract
    and exorcise these ghouls
Hey, a little mixture of you, some mushrooms and greens
    will have us floating in ecstasy
Never mind the devil is a headache baby
Its OK if you want to pop one or two
    before I viciously devour the beast out of your body
I stared at you, gaze and amazed by the wonders of your moon
As you opens both cheeks up showing me
    a different point of view
I can tell you're happy the way your cracks and crevices
    are smirking at me
As I arrive closer both doors shining, glistening also glad
    to finally see me
You'll let me break in, but you enjoy me teasing, touching
    and caressing my way in, slowly
When I walk and slide my index and middle finger
    circularly over it
Casually with the palm of my hands feeling around
    the meat of it
The smell is exotic you know I can't help it
I want to squeeze, rub, kiss, slap and bite on it

Gently inserting my thumb in it while rubbing the bottom of it
Looking at you from the side, sweating moaning, giggling
      of course you like it
Gasping for air running out of breath like you want to forfeit
I put you on all fours like a cow
You like it when I'm using my other hand to milk it

I usually don't like my steak medium rare,
      but you're busting it
And I'm tearing it wide open, admiring it
Gushing and dripping out your juices and cream
I'm even more turned on, call me an animal, cannibalist
      or a fucking machine
I go on, and on and on even when I see waters
      pouring out your holy streams
It's turning to a slaughter house, and I haven't even
      used my biggest tool yet
It's becoming a crime scene now; your whole body
      is gooey and wet
Like we are in a real hollywood movie set,
Lights, camer,a action looks like the sun has already long set
We going to have a magical and memorable night
      you won't regret
Listen a blissful moment with me can have you feel
      like you're possessed
In case you don't remember when you get a headache
      or when you're stressed
Encrypted in your memory as reminder of me,
      to make you happy baby, not upset

Frantzy Civil

I'll keep the camera running, capturing every moment
    without missing a sec
All rights of the footage belongs to you if,
    by any chance, you forget
Hey, better yet post it on social media whenever you
    want to go viral on the internet
Your new man might hate me when he finds out
    how much you love pain
He thought you only enjoy soft, magical moments under the rain
Hey, it happens, or maybe you were not
    that sexually in tune with him
Never mind him and how much he thinks
    you were twin flame,
Police might come arrest me, thinking you
    were being restrained
It's OK I know they want to hold me captive,
    but secretly they want to learn game
Even the judge will be baffled, how you were pulling me closer
    smiling and crying
Tears of joy, not knowing a blissful moment
    in ecstasy   with me is amazing

Frantzy Civil

All Aboard
All Welcome In

From the opening of the elevator doors,
    me and my friend's chuckling didn't go no further
As we looked down, we saw what looked like bird crap
    mixed with yellow watery peanut butter
    close to the middle of the doorway,
    which could not be ignored!
But it smells like another old sick patient's defecation
    stinking up one of the hospital's floor
"Are you serious bro…?!' was the first words that came
    out my friend *'Kleeno*'s mouth for sure
I stop abruptly, his face looking somewhat like a whale
    that had died offshore
We both shake our head with despair..,
    as we slide swiftly by the corridor!
I start imagining what if we were eating,
    or were with a few people together
    walking out with a stroller
Or say a suitcase seeing a splat of that
    a few feet away out from the elevator!
"How did that happen," thinking out loud,
    "probably the night before… "
At least we didn't witness how it happened live in action
You wouldn't imagine
    what I saw a few months prior to this
    at another train station (sigh)

One afternoon in the train, almost full
    with people standing for the ride as we left the station.
Believe it or not, I've witnessed this elderly man
    seemed like he's around sixty years of age
        without any hesitation..,
he pulled down his pants, holding the train's loose bar-rail
    in one of those weird crouch positions!
    he began to unload his dump,
    in the bridge of the two doors of the train's car
        as we pass numerous stations!
Even witness him using a paper tissue to wipe down,
    'mmhm that's an awkward situation'
Kleeno asked quickly, *"Now you're shitting me!*
    So, he didn't even wash his hands..?"
My eyes glare at him, with an eyebrow starting to take elevation
    like Rocky Johnson.
Anyways to continue the story,
    he opened the door on the other side
        sat down for a few seconds
In 3 more minutes he returned for round two..,
    and I swear to life, it seems like a few seconds
Kleeno inserted a quick comment, *"Bro,*
    you be witnessing and running into
    too many distorting situations"
Hahaha, anyways the shuttle train is here.

Frantzy Civil

We wait, till everybody leaves, sit down
        although our stop was only few stops from here,
As I sat down still in shock,
            I noticed this elderly man
        looking like an all black buccaneer
Sitting,
            looks like a scarecrow
    with mostly garbage bags covering his body!
Plus, the same sick patient's defecation scent
        is overcrowding the place not so heavily
Mmhm my eyes open like a hawk hunting...
           'no way could it be...'
We both look at each other like mmhm
        again we smirk but couldn't get angry
Ok! We left and walk up and around
        go on the other pathway down a few levels quickly
Soon as we got in the other train,
        the operator mentioned from the trains speaker
            we all have to leave
We will have to go get the bus or something because suddenly
        somebody let that mood carry them
           somewhere dark and violent,
  Probably to death the way he spoke, so loudly
"What we do now.., I ain't trying to be super crowded in a bus?"

First,

We can take the same pathway to catch same shuttle
                further next station
          for another train which is the same distance,
       but on the other side from our destination
"Igh let's go, it's just a little wait again.,"
                as we wait, I'm there pondering
My adventures so far in this city sometimes be funny,
           but at the same time very concerning
Why it seems like in our community elderly people
                are miserably dying,
         plus plenty are homeless in one of
            the world's richest city herein?
I stop baffling as I peep pennies or coins flying and dropping
              onto tracks, like a wishing well,
Just hope he stays away from jumping in,
          then I'll have too truly wishing him well (Sigh…)
'Today I've encountered one of the most phenomenal situations
          in these public transportations for sure'
This city's public transportation seems like
         one of the most easy access places to enter
        either wait for somebody to swipe you in,
              ask the teller,
            jump the turnstile
          and/or ask an officer.
Depends, but it seems like in NYC we all have access to travel
In public transportation, not having any money
             isn't as much of an obstacle!

Colophon

Wider Perspectives Publishing regrets to have to announce that the ongoing Colophon page, used to tout artists published in books from WPP, has to be reworked. This is due to the growing library of fine writers coming out of, or even into, the Hampton Roads area of Virginia.

Donna Burnett-Robinson
Faith Griffin
Se'Mon-Michelle Rosser
Lisa M. Kendrick
Cassandra IsFree
Nich (Nicholis Williams)
Samantha Geovjian Clarke
Natalie Morison-Uzzle
Gus Woodward II
Patsy Bickerstaff
Edith Blake
Jack Cassada
DezzDaniel Garwood
Jada Hollingsworth
Tabetha Moon House
Travis Hailes- Virgo, thePoet
Nick Marickovich
Grey Hues
Rivers Raye
Madeline Garcia
Chichi Iwuorie
Symay Rhodes
Tanya Cunningham-Jones
    (Scientific Eve)
Terra Leigh
Raymond M. Simmons
Samantha Borders-Shoemaker
Taz Weysweete'
Jade Leonard
Darean Polk
Bobby K.
    (The Poor Man's Poet)

J. Scott Wilson (TEECH!)
Charles Wilson
Gloria Darlene Mann
Neil Spirtas
Jorge Mendez & JT Williams
Sarah Eileen Williams
Stephanie Diana (Noftz)
Shanya – Lady S.
Jason Brown (Drk Mtr)
Ken Sutton
Kailyn Rae Sasso
Crickyt J. Expression

Catherine TL Hodges
Kent Knowlton
Linda Spence-Howard
Maria April C.
Tony Broadway
Zach Crowe

Mark Willoughby
Martina Champion
... and others to come soon.

the Hampton Roads
   Artistic Collective (757
   Perspectives) &
The Poet's Domain
are all WPP literary journals in cooperation with Scientific Eve or Live Wire Press

Check for those artists on FaceBook, Instagram, the Virginia Poetry Online channel on YouTube, and other social media.

www.ingramcontent.com/pod-product-compliance
Lightning Source LLC
Chambersburg PA
CBHW031219090426
42736CB00009B/986